Heartfelt Inspirations

D0766994

Happy Cats

Hervé Desbois

MODUS VIVENDI

© 2002 Les Publications Modus Vivendi Inc.

Publications Modus Vivendi Inc.
3859, Laurentian Autoroute
Laval (Québec)
Canada
H7L 3H7

Layout: Modus Vivendi
Cover Design: Marc Alain

ISBN: 2-89523-107-9

Legal deposit, 4th trimester 2002
Bibliothèque nationale du Québec
Bibliothèque nationale du Canada

Canadä We acknowledge the financial support of the Government of Canada through the Book Publishing Industry Development Program (BPIDP) for our publishing activities.

Government of Québec — Tax credit for book publishing—
Administered by SODEC

Heartfelt Inspirations

Happy Cats

Hervé Desbois

MODUS VIVENDI

REFLECTIONS ON CATS

Renoir, Steinlen, and Toulouse-Lautrec have drawn or painted felines, while a number of writers were lost in admiration for the beasts: Colette, Baudelaire, Victor Hugo, Sainte-Beuve, Taine, Théophile Gautier, Prévert, etc. Others, like Ronsard, and Ambroise Paré, on their part seemed not to be very fond of them.

Since the beginning of time, cats have fascinated human beings. We love or we hate the animal, but rarely are we indifferent to it. Some are repelled to be in its presence while others cannot help going to stroke one as soon as they see it. I have even know a woman who lived in Africa, and who didn't fear snakes or scorpions, but who was overcome with uncontrollable panic in the presence of a cat!

Mythology and legends about cats cover the passages of time, in the East as well as in the West, from the Antiquity up until today.

A lot was said and written about cats. Mysteries, love, myths, and witchcraft, here are a few proverbs and thoughts that glorify or curse them, a few bits of knowledge that will inform or surprise you, a few excerpts from writings that will make you laugh, or smile.

And may cat lovers forgive me for not having repeated all that has been said or written about this "feline god."

HERVÉ DESBOIS

I have studied many philosophers and many cats. The wisdom of cats is infinitely superior.

HIPPOLYTE TAINE

Cat chronicles : When a domestic cat died a natural death in Egypt, its human companions shaved their eyebrows and cried for hours.

LAURETTE THERRIEN

As a house cat, it's my duty to ignore you.

GARFIELD

After dark all cats are leopards.

NATIVE AMERICAN PROVERB

The cat will mew, and dog will have his day.

WILLIAM SHAKESPEARE

After scolding one's cat one looks into its face and is seized by the ugly suspicion that it understood every word. And has filed it for reference.

CHARLOTTE GRAY

Buffon mistreated the cat, I am working on its rehabilitation. I hope to make it a properly honest animal, in today's fashion.

CHATEAUBRIAND

That way look, my infant, lo!
What a pretty baby-show!
See the kitten on the wall,
Sporting with the leaves that fall.

WILLIAM WORDSWORTH

No matter how much cats fight, there always
seems to be plenty of kittens.

ABRAHAM LINCOLN

It is difficult to catch a black cat in a dark room,
especially when it isn't there.

CHINESE PROVERB

What a shame that my cat
Joined the land of the dead
To stay clear of her paw
No rat ever ran enough

MÉNARD

Cat chronicles : Across all of history and the customs of man, cats have always been a symbol of femininity.

LAURETTE THERRIEN

Cats have something royal about them: they demand everything from you without doing anything themselves.

HERVÉ DESBOIS

Cat! who hast pass'd thy grand climacteric,
How many mice and rats hast in thy days
Destroy'd?—How many tit bits stolen? Gaze
With those bright languid segments green,
            and prick
Those velvet ears—but pr'ythee do not stick
Thy latent talons in me—and upraise
Thy gentle mew—and tell me all thy frays
Of fish and mice, and rats and tender chick.
Nay, look not down, nor lick thy dainty wrists—
For all the wheezy asthma,—and for all
Thy tail's tip is nick'd off—and though the fists
Of many a maid have given thee many a maul,
Still is that fur as soft as when the lists
In youth thou enter'dst on glass-bottled wall.

JOHN KEATS

With the qualities of cleanliness, affection, patience, dignity, and courage that cats have, how many of us, I ask you, would be capable of becoming cats?

FERNAND MÉRY

A cat sees no good reason why it should obey another animal, even if it does stand on two legs.

SARAH THOMPSON

Crossing a brook while holding a cat in your arms is bad luck.

FRENCH PROVERB

You only have to meet a cat's eyes in order to measure the depth of the enigmas that each of the flakes in its eyes sets down for the brave human beings that we are.

JACQUES LAURENT

A dog will flatter you but you have to flatter the cat.

GEORGE MIKES

Cat chronicles: In the time of the Inquisition, the fear of cats seizes Europe. Almost everywhere, women and men are subject to torture and are burned for having looked after or taken in a cat.

LAURETTE THERRIEN

I wish for a home
A woman with her reason
A cat walking among the books
Friends in all seasons.

GUILLAUME APOLLINAIRE

He who likes a cat likes all cats.
He who likes his dog likes no other.

ROLAND TOPOR

No amount of time can erase the memory of a
good cat, and no amount of masking tape can
ever totally remove his fur from your couch.

LEO DWORKEN

There's no need for a piece of sculpture in a home that has a cat.

WESLEY BATES

In its eyes, I am but another object furnishing his territory.

HERVÉ DESBOIS

… Deshoulières is always ungrateful
To those caught by her beautiful eyes
But her heart, like that of a mouse
Is caught… by a cat!

MADAME DESHOULIÈRES

Cat chronicles: Who were "Chanoine" and "Gavroche"? Two of the many cats that occupied a place of choice in the life of the renowned writer Victor Hugo.

LAURETTE THERRIEN

Cats know how to obtain food without labour, shelter without confinement, and love without penalties.

W. L. GEORGE

Everything I know I learned from my cat: When you're hungry, eat. When you're tired, nap in a sunbeam. When you go to the vet's, pee on your owner.

GARY SMITH

Where the mouse makes fun of the cat... there is a hole.

PORTUGUESE PROVERB

When you parade with insolence
And when you mew with no restraint
Demanding complete obedience
And infinite virtue
In answering with diligence
To the urgency of filling your belly

HERVÉ DESBOIS

Cats and superstition: Until the end of the XIXth century, Basque farmers believed that witches appeared in the guise of black cats.

EXCERPT FROM LE GRAND LIVRE DES CHATS

Man is civilised as long as he understands the cat.

GEORGE BERNARD SHAW

Do you know Maneki-neko, the little Japanese she-cat with the right paw raised at eye-level, who coaxes and bewitches, brings happiness and ensures luck?

LAURETTE THERRIEN

Cats are animals of habit. Comfort and security are at the top of their priority list. They don't have the sense of change as humans do.

EXCERPT FROM LE GRAND LIVRE DES CHATS

This singular animal seemed in pantomime to be comforting his master and offering advice, which was finally acted upon, for Mac pulled off his boots, helped the little beast into them, and gave him a bag; then, kissing his paw, with a hopeful gesture, the creature retired, purring so successfully that there was a general cry of "Cat, puss, boots!"

LOUISA M. ALCOTT
EIGHT COUSINS

Never put a cat in charge of watching the hens.
ENGLISH PROVERB

The Cat only grinned when it saw Alice. It looked good-natured, she thought: still it had VERY long claws and a great many teeth, so she felt that it ought to be treated with respect.

LEWIS CARROLL

Cats are distant, discreet, impeccably clean, and they know how to keep quiet. Is there need for more to be good company?

MARIE LECZINSKA

If you want to see what others will not be able to see, rub your eyes with a cat dropping and white hen grease, mixed together with wine.

HERMES

A cat is a cat.

SPANISH PROVERB

Cats are never bored. They always have hair to clean or a nap to take.

HERVÉ DESBOIS

There was a crooked man,
And he went a crooked mile
He found a crooked sixpence
Against a crooked stile
He bought a crooked cat,
Which caught a crooked mouse
And they all lived together
In a little crooked house.

NURSERY RHYME

For my part, I have known absolutely infernal and untouchable female cats, and male cats that were sweet and nice enough to make you melt.

Excerp from Vivre Avec Son Chat

I like, in the cat, this independent and almost ungrateful nature that makes it not become attached to anyone, this indifference with which it goes from sitting rooms to its native gutters... The cat lives alone. It has no need for society. It obeys only when it cares to, pretends to be asleep in order to see better, and scratches all it can scratch.

Chateaubriand

A cat bitten once by a snake will fear even a rope.

PROVERB

Cat chronicles: In the time of the Inquisition, The Hammer of Witches, a manual listing all of Satan's tricks, curiously contains very few accusations against cats.

LAURETTE THERRIEN

God is really only another artist. He invented the giraffe, the elephant and the cat. He has no real style, He just goes on trying other things.

PABLO PICASSO

Cats sleep anywhere, any table, any chair.
Top of piano, window-ledge, in the middle, on
the edge.
Open draw, empty shoe, anybody's lap will do.
Fitted in a cardboard box, in the cupboard
with your frocks.
Anywhere! They don't care! Cats sleep any-
where!

ELEANOR FARJEON

You don't raise cats, cats raise you.

JIM DAVIS

A cat first falls into a light sleep, then sinks into
a deep sleep, interrupted by periods of light
sleep. Rolled up into a ball, it often snores...

LAURETTE THERRIEN

Laziness has its advantages, including not having to name them.

GARFIELD

Cat chronicles: It is believed that Egyptians were the first to domesticate cats, around the XVIIIth dynasty.

LAURETTE THERRIEN

Cats are notoriously sore losers. Coming in second best, especially to someone as poorly co-ordinated as a human being, grates their sensibility.

STEPHEN BAKER

The dog is a group animal, which hunts in packs, like the wolf and most wild canines. Hence the dog's total submission to man, which it considers to be the leader of the pack (better than the other way around for you!), and hence the relative independence of the cat, which is still not domesticated, let's remember.

PIERRE DARMANGEAT

We cannot doubt the intelligence of cats: they know very well who feeds them.

HERVÉ DESBOIS

Before cats, weasels were in charge of hunting for rats on ships.

LAURETTE THERRIEN

Gutter cat
You give yourself airs
Alley cat
You go wenching at night
House cat
Wherever you go
You are the king, I know
The cat has too much spirit to have no heart.

ERNEST MENAUL

The naming of cats is a difficult matter. It isn't just one of your holiday games. You may think at first I'm mad as a hatter. When I tell you a cat must have three different names...

T.S. ELIOT

A cat may go to a monastery, but it still remains a cat.

AFRICAN PROVERB

Cats are rather delicate creatures and they are subject to a lot of ailments, but I never heard of one who suffered from insomnia.

JOSEPH WOOD CRUTCH

You aren't born lazy, it's an art you acquire, an art you refine, a little bit like poetry, dance, or music.

GARFIELD

"It's raining cats and dogs" or it's raining so hard you can hardly see in front of you.

ENGLISH EXPRESSION

It is midnight, the farm is asleep.
Alone, opening her great golden eyes,
Close to the hearth, the cat keeps watch.

FRANÇOIS FABIÉ

Cat chronicles: Stockholm, in Sweden, is recognised as being the cat capital of the world. If one of them gets lost, the police calls out to all, the press talks about it, it is immediately taken in and adopted.

LAURETTE THERRIEN

I do nothing quickly, except falling asleep.

GARFIELD

If I die before my cat, I want a little of my ashes put in his food so I can live inside him.

DREW BARRYMORE

Cats are a mysterious kind of folk. There is more passing in their minds than we are aware of.

SIR WALTER SCOTT

Most beds sleep up to six cats. Ten cats without the owner.

STEPHEN BAKER

If animals could speak the dog would be a blundering outspoken fellow, but the cat would have the rare grace of never saying a word too much.

MARK TWAIN

How to explain to a cat that we can be so different, yet still be friends? And most importantly, how to explain it when we don't speak the same language?

BERNADETTE RENAUD
LE CHAT DE L'ORATOIRE

The cat is nature's Beauty.

FRENCH PROVERB

A greedy cat makes the maid attentive.

PROVENÇAL PROVERB

Dogs come when they're called; cats take a message and get back to you later.

MARY BLY

Kitten, lovely kitten
Hurry up and fatten up
After the summer months
You will go out to hunt

LAURETTE THERRIEN

Who knows what is hidden and what happens behind those eyes watching us.

HERVÉ DESBOIS

Cats always know whether people like or dislike them. They do not always care enough to do anything about it.

WINIFRED CARRIÈRE

You see with joy a lover to his demise
Yet for a cat you shed your tears
This bizarre contrast, Iris, does not please me
And I am indignant about your foolish alarms...

LIOTTARD

"The cat is in the clock", or there's a running
battle in the household.

FLEMISH PROVERB

Every day, I consume each of the four food
groups: breakfast, lunch, dinner, and snacks.

GARFIELD

Here rests a pretty cat
Her mistress who loved nothing
Loved her to the point of madness
Why say it?
It's plain to see!

ANONYMOUS

Her majesty lady cat
Will turn her back to you
If she doesn't want your company

This four-legged ladyship
Will look at you haughtily
Even if she sees you from below

In her kingdom
Cats rule
In her kingdom
Cats are kings

HERVÉ DESBOIS

Your cat's behaviour depends essentially on you. Be tender, and it will also be. Be violent, and it will run away from you. If you have shifting moods, your cat will be neurotic, not knowing which saint-cat to turn to when approaching you.

EXCERPT FROM VIVRE AVEC SON CHAT

Cat chronicles: During the High Middle Ages, cloisters, abbeys and monasteries were infested with rodents. Cats received an extraordinary welcome, because they were counted on to exterminate rats and mice.

LAURETTE THERRIEN

The mathematical probability of a common cat doing exactly as it pleases is the one scientific absolute in the world.

LYNN M. OSBAND

What do I really need? An attentive ear, a warm heart, a tender look, a few laughing opportunities, a cat or a dog, maybe, is enough to make me happy.

JEROME K. JEROME

Fat is a funny thing. You never lose it where you would like to.

GARFIELD

Cats seem to go on the principle that it never does any harm to ask for what you want.

JOSEPH WOOD KRUTCH

How we behave toward cats here below determines our status in heaven.

ROBERT A. HEINLEIN

We cannot say that cats, even though they live in our homes, are pets; even the most docile do not let themselves be brought under subjection.

BUFFON

Intelligence in the cat is underrated.

LOUIS WAIN

When the cat is away, the mice will play.

FRENCH PROVERB

When dreaming, they assume the noble attitudes
Of the great sphinxs stretched out in solitude,
Which seem to sleep in an endless dream.

CHARLES BAUDELAIRE

I don't envy my cat's life, nor does it envy mine. At least, I think not.

HERVÉ DESBOIS

If a cat did not put a firm paw down now and then, how could his human remain possessed.

WINIFRED CARRIÈRE

Cats pacify the soul. A cat has no worries, because it thinks intuitively.

PAL GERHARD OLSEN

He who insults you only insults himself.
However, my lawyers believe otherwise.

GARFIELD

If cats wore gloves, they would not catch any mice.

HINDU PROVERB

Cats are eternal children: they eat, they play, they sleep, and what do they give you in return? Worries, but moments of pure happiness too.

HERVÉ DESBOIS

A cat is there when you call her — if she doesn't have something better to do.

BILL ADLER

Cats can be cooperative when something feels good, which, to a cat, is the way everything is supposed to feel as much of the time as possible.

ROGER CARAS

And perfect is the peace, and more peaceful still in its serenity, the sleepy cat exudes silence with its breath (…)

RAY BRADBURY

I would gladly add that the more vivacious, curious, enterprising, even infernal a kitten is, the more chances you have of laughing to death in its company.

EXCERPT FROM VIVRE AVEC SON CHAT

Dogs have masters, cats have servants.

DAVE BARRY

Prowling his own quiet backyard or asleep by the fire, he is still only a whisker away from the wilds.

JEAN BURDEN

The smallest feline is a masterpiece.

LEONARDO DA VINCI

Cat chronicles: In Ancient Egypt, the cat, after the vulture, was the sacred animal par excellence.

LAURETTE THERRIEN

The cat's motto: whatever you did, always try to make them believe it's the dog's fault.

JEFF VALDEZ

The real gentleman is the one who always calls a cat a cat. Even when he trips on it and falls.

MARCEL ACHARD

"Busier than a one-eyed cat watching nine rat holes", or someone who has too many things to do.

ENGLISH EXPRESSION

A house without cats is like a fish tank without fish.

JEAN-LOUIS HUE

A charmer
He sways and snakes by
He purrs and coils up
He stretches
And rolls up
Into a ball
A fighter
He defies and threatens
He confronts, tenacious
He arches his back
Bares his fangs
What an animal!
But how human he is
This feline!

HERVÉ DESBOIS

Cat chronicles: In the middle of the XXth century, many marine insurance companies refuse to pay for merchandise damages caused by rodents if there aren't any cats aboard the ships.

LAURETTE THERRIEN

The Chartreux loves following its master like a little... dog. But beware of open doors: it's good at running away!

PIERRE DARMANGEAT

I'm famished, therefore I am.

GARFIELD

The gingham dog went "bow-wow-wow!"
And the calico cat replied "mee-ow!"
The air was littered, an hour or so,
With bits of gingham and calico,
While the old Dutch clock in the chimney-place
Up with its hands before its face,
For it always dreaded a family row!

EUGENE FIELD

THE DUEL

There are few things in life more heart-warming
than to be welcomed by a cat.

TAY HOHOFF

Women and cats inside the house, men and dogs
outside the house.

ALSATIAN PROVERB

Cat chronicles: In 1727, Paradis de Moncrif published his Histoire et coutumes des chats (History and Customs of Cats). The work opened to its author the doors to the Académie.

LAURETTE THERRIEN

A house without a cat, how empty it is!

BERTRAND VAC

According to me, nothing beats Sundays... the only day when laziness is required.

GARFIELD

I believe cats to be spirits come to earth. A cat, I am sure, could walk on a cloud without coming through.

JULES VERNE

He is quiet, he is small, he is black
From the ears to the tip of his tail
He can creep through the tiniest crack
He can walk on the narrowest rail
He can pick any card from a pack
He is equally cunning with dice
He is always deceiving you into believing
That he's only hunting for mice

ANDREW LLOYD WEBBER

CATS

Better to feed your cat than to feed the rat.

FRENCH PROVERB

There are no ordinary cats.

COLETTE

The cat and the writer make up the perfect couple.

ANNY DUPEREY

The cat that frightens the mice away is as good as the cat that eats them.

GERMAN PROVERB

In a fire, between a Rembrandt and a cat, I would save the cat.

ALBERTO GIACOMETTI

With many an ardent wish,
She stretched in vain to reach the prize.
What female heart can gold despise?
What cat's averse to fish?

THOMAS GRAY

Most cats, when they are out want to be in, and visa versa, and often simultaneously.

LOUIS J. CAMUTI

I have a good way of judging my employers: they are civilised if they have a cat on the sofa and a teddy bear on the bed.

CONCHA SUARES

We should be careful to get out of an experience only the wisdom that is in it and stop there, lest we be like the cat that sits down on a hot stove-lid. She will never sit down on a hot stove-lid again, and that is well; but also she will never sit down on a cold one anymore.

MARK TWAIN

I wish I could write as mysterious as a cat.

EDGAR ALLAN POE

The cat seldom interferes with other people's rights. His intelligence keeps him from doing many of the fool things that complicate life.

CARL VAN VECHTEN

"I didn't know that Cheshire cats always grinned; in fact, I didn't know that cats COULD grin. -They all can," said the Duchess; "and most of 'em do."

LEWIS CARROLL

But I tell you, a cat needs a name that's particular,
A name that's peculiar, and more dignified,
Else how can he keep up his tail perpendicular,
Or spread out his whiskers, or cherish his pride?

T.S. ELIOT

Cat chronicles: In the xth century, a person who steals or kills a cat on his neighbour's land must pay him back with a sheep and its lamb, or pay a fine equalling the quantity of wheat necessary to completely cover the cat's body, held by the tip of the tail, its nose brushing the ground.

LAURETTE THERRIEN

Of all the animals, only the cat reaches a contemplative life.

ANDREW LANG

One of the most striking differences between a cat and a lie is that a cat only has nine lives.

MARK TWAIN

Little by little, cats become the soul of the house.

JEAN COCTEAU

Mother-in-law and daughter-in-law in the same house are like two cats in a bag.

YIDDISH PROVERB

Three things never arrive fast enough: birthdays, Christmas… and the pizza delivery man.

GARFIELD

Women are like cats that always fall back on their feet.

PERSIAN PROVERB

Even overweight, cats instinctively know the cardinal rule: when fat, arrange yourself in slim poses.

JOHN WEITZ

They say the test of literary power is whether a man can write an inscription. I say: Can he name a kitten?

SAMUEL BUTLER

When your dog jumps on your bed, it's because it loves your company. When your cat jumps on your bed, it's because it loves your bed.

ALISHA EVERETT

Cat chronicles: Against rats, cats have always surpassed all traps and poisons. They were even superior to ratters, because more discreet and much more patient.

LAURETTE THERRIEN

Cats do care. For example they know instinctively what time we have to be at work in the morning and they wake us up twenty minutes before the alarm goes off.

MICHAEL NELSON

The cat went here and there
And the moon spun round like a top,
And the nearest kin of the moon,
The creeping cat, looked up.
Black Minnaloushe stared at the moon,
For, wander and wail as he would,
The pure cold light in the sky
Troubled his animal blood.
Minnaloushe runs in the grass
Lifting his delicate feet.
Do you dance, Minnaloushe, do you dance?
When two close kindred meet,
What better than call a dance?

WILLIAM BUTLER YEATS

THE CAT AND THE MOON

If I prefer cats to dogs, it's because there are no police cats.

JEAN COCTEAU

Do not believe that a cat breaks everything on purpose, no: it is only living out its crazy young cat's life, developing with all the more enthusiasm as it is happy in your home, and learning all it needs to.

EXCERPT FROM VIVRE AVEC SON CHAT

If the cats guard the goats, who will catch the mice?

FRENCH PROVERB

A meow massages the heart.

STUART MCMILLAN

Cats are the ultimate narcissists. You can tell this by all the time they spend on personal grooming. Dogs aren't like this. A dog's idea of personal grooming is to roll in a dead fish.

JAMES GORMAN

Cat: soft automaton supplied by nature to receive kicks when things go wrong in the family circle.

AMBROSE BIERCE

A sleeping cat does not hunt.

FRENCH PROVERB

Those who play with cats must expect to be scratched.

MIGUEL DE CERVANTÈS

People that hate cats will come back as mice in their next life.

FAITH RESNICK

A cat has absolute emotional honesty: human beings, for one reason or another, may hide their feelings, but a cat does not.

ERNEST HEMINGWAY

Let's never forget who the centre of the world is here.

GARFIELD

How sad tomcats are,
To be no more on the knees
That provided them with such a soft bed!

RAOUL GINESTE

At night, all cats are grey.

RUSSIAN PROVERB

Come and hear
This delightful and tasteful concert
Magnificent are its tunes
Come and hear my tomcats.

A CAT SHOW IN THE XVIIth CENTURY

Cat chronicles: Our domestic cat has as most
probable ancestor the African wild cat, Felis sil-
veris lybica, originating from North-East Africa.

LAURETTE THERRIEN

Women and cats do what they want, and men and dogs should relax and get used to the idea.

ROBERT HEINLEIN

Sleeping cat or playing cat
Big black cat or tiny orange cat
To each his cat, to each his preference!

ANONYMOUS

In the beginning, God created man, but seeing him so feeble, He gave him the cat.

WARREN ECKSTEIN

All cats are mortals, Socrates is mortal, therefore Socrates is a cat.

EUGÈNE IONESCO

The cat stares at the man; it is worried. It feels its friend's suffering.

BERNADETTE RENAUD
LE CHAT DE L'ORATOIRE

The Abyssinian cat is the king of sulking! It is not mean, loves you to death, and expects to be loved in return, otherwise it sulks...

PIERRE DARMANGEAT

If the rat put on breeches, cats are the ones to take them off.

AFRICAN PROVERB

There is no more intrepid explorer than a kitten.

JULES CHAMPFLEURY

If in discipline matters your cat is a recurrent offender, a squirt of water will set it straight.

Excerpt from
GUIDE VÉTÉRINAIRE DES CHIENS ET DES CHATS

The rat will not move as long as the cat's eyes are shining.

MADAGASCAR PROVERB

Cat chronicles:
Before Islam, Arabs also adored a golden cat; the Koran only confirms the respect owed to the cat, advising not to chase it out of the mosque or the tent.

LAURETTE THERRIEN

It's possible to be worn out without working so hard.

GARFIELD

Argumentative or independent spirit? Why must they run away from you when you approach them, and jump out at you when you are not expecting them?

HERVÉ DESBOIS

It's for her own good that the cat purrs.

IRISH PROVERB

The Chinese see the time in the eyes of cats.

BAUDELAIRE

Before a cat will condescend
To treat you as a trusted friend
Some little token of esteem is needed,
*   like a dish of cream*
And you might now and then supply
Some caviar or Strassburg pie
Some potted grouse or salmon paste
He's sure to have his personal taste

ANDREW LLOYD WEBBER

A man has to work so hard so that something of
his personality stays alive. A tomcat has it so
easy, he has only to spray and his presence is
there for years on rainy days.

ALBERT EINSTEIN

Cat chronicles: Did you know that cats are great fans of stuffed olives? Try and see.

LAURETTE THERRIEN

The Skogatt (a.k.a. "Cat of the Norwegian Forests") is affectionate with its master, but doesn't bear long petting sessions: held against its will, it can scratch!

VIVRE AVEC SON CHAT

A repressed cat becomes a lion.

ENGLISH PROVERB

If you really want to know what love and marriage can be like, have at home a couple of cats.

ALDOUS HUXLEY

Cat chronicles: In Greece, monks of Mount Athos, although very hostile towards the opposite sex, made an exception for female cats, concerned as they were to fight against their littlest hosts.

LAURETTE THERRIEN

Permission given once, habit taken on forever.

ANONYMOUS

"Pas de chat" and "entrechats", could it be that felines are also good dancers?

HERVÉ DESBOIS

If your cat surprises you and jumps with all its claws out, surprise it too, by blowing on him with a pump or with something else.

Excerpt from
GUIDE VÉTÉRINAIRE DES CHIENS ET DES CHATS

One reason we admire cats is for their proficiency in one-upmanship. They always seem to come out on top, no matter what they are doing, or pretend they do.

BARBARA WEBSTER

He purred and purred
Gave three mews
Came to rest on his side
And gave my fingers a lick

LAURETTE THERRIEN

The cat is an unfaithful domestic we only keep
because we have no choice.

BUFFON

A black cat I am
In Lithuania I live.
Little devil, they blame me
As, to those who sell their souls to me
Goods and money do I give
"Aitvaras" I am called.

ADAPTATION OF A LITHUANIAN LEGEND

Sleeping makes me hungry, and eating makes me sleepy.
Life is well made.

GARFIELD

Cat chronicles: In the xth century, while rats run havoc in crops and pantries, a cat is worth double its price after the death of a simple mouse.

LAURETTE THERRIEN

Cats are a tonic, they are a laugh, they are a cuddle, they are at least pretty just about all of the time and beautiful some of the time.

ROGER CARAS

If you are worthy of its affection, a cat will become your friend, but never your slave.

THÉOPHILE GAUTIER

Cats exist in our world to refute the dogma that all things were created in order to serve man.

FROQUEVIELLE

A dog, a cat, is a heart with fur around it.

BRIGITTE BARDOT

Beware of people who dislike cats.

IRISH PROVERB

Of all domestic animals the cat is the most expressive. His face is capable of showing a wide range of expressions. His tail is a mirror of his mind. His gracefulness is surpassed only by his agility. And, along with all these, he has a sense of humour.

WALTER CHANDOHA

Playing? In the sense of wasting energy for no apparent reason? I can play in my sleep!

GARFIELD

You will always be lucky if you know how to make friends with strange cats.

COLONIAL PROVERB

Her function is to sit and be admired.

GEORGINA STRICKLAND GATES

This happy lass has shifting moods. Even the most adorable individual is capable of rebellion and sulking. Because cats do sulk!

EXCERPT FROM VIVRE AVEC SON CHAT

*When I play with my cat, who knows if I am not
a greater pastime for him than he is for me.*

ANONYMOUS

*I was called Mafdet
The lady of the castle of life.
I was an ancient goddess
Of the first dynasty
In Ancient Egypt.
Behind my feline appearance
Scorpions I destroyed
And snakes I did not fear.
Against their bites, I was invoked.*

HERVÉ DESBOIS

ADAPTATION OF EGYPTIAN MYTHOLOGY

Of all the animal species, cats are the most self-centred.
Are there other species?

GARFIELD

Cat chronicles: They claim that cats were first brought into Japan in the VIth century, like Buddhism. Temples relied on them to protect the manuscripts about ethics against mice.

LAURETTE THERRIEN

What is more beautiful? The feline's movements or its peace?

ELIZABETH HAMILTON

To "let the cat out of the bag", or when a secret is no longer a secret...

ENGLISH EXPRESSION

If a violent fire erupts anywhere in Egypt, people will not be worried about the fire, but about their cats.

HERODOTUS

If you shamefully misuse a cat once she will always maintain a dignified reserve toward you afterward. You will never get her full confidence again.

MARK TWAIN

This faculty that cats have of travelling for kilometres and coming back home months later remains a mystery.

LAURETTE THERRIEN

The cat could very well be man's best friend but would never stoop to admitting it.

DOUG LARSON

A dried fish cannot be used as a cat's pillow.

CHINESE PROVERB

No one owns a cat! It's more like a long-term loan.

GARFIELD

Why don't you go about your business
Take care of something urgent
You have other things to do
You can't "wait for the cat to jump."

HERVÉ DESBOIS
FREE ADAPTATION OF A SAYING

A cat is independent, but if it decides you are "its thing", it will never leave you a moment's rest.

LAURETTE THERRIEN

Moreover, if it gets some sunshine, you are making it very happy: cats love basking in its warmth.

EXCERPT FROM VIVRE AVEC SON CHAT

Cat chronicles: In the beginning of the XXth century, in Denmark, the ratter cat is officially a "state employee" for its role in post offices and prisons, museums, libraries, and firehouses.

LAURETTE THERRIEN

Cat-flap: it's the cat's door built on your own house door and which allows your cat to come inside its home, or your home, depending on the point of view.

HERVÉ DESBOIS

Cats are fanatical about cleanliness!

PIERRE DARMANGEAT

The Cat and the sun:
The cat opened its eyes
The sun entered them
The cat closed its eyes
The sun remained in them

That is why at night
When the cat wakes up
I can see in the dark
Two pieces of sunshine.

MAURICE CARÊME

Cats' hearing apparatus is built to allow the human voice to easily go in one ear and out the other.

STEPHEN BAKER

Cat chronicles: In France, in the XIth century, cats are so well thought of that they appear in inheritance inventories.

LAURETTE THERRIEN

Cats are kindly masters, just so long as you remember your place.

PAUL GRAY

"All right," said the Cat; and this time it vanished quite slowly, beginning with the end of the tail, end ending with the grin, which remained some time after the rest of it had gone. "Well! I've often seen a cat without a grin," thought Alice; "but a grin without a cat! It's the most curious thing I ever saw in my life!"

LEWIS CARROLL

Don't hold me any which way
I you don't want to feel my teeth
Or my claws in your skin,
If you truly want to please me
A hand under my breast will go,
Another my hind paws will hold.

HERVÉ DESBOIS

When cats smooth out the backs of their ears,
rain or a storm are not far away.

LAURETTE THERRIEN

A cat seems to think only of itself, to love only
under conditions set by itself, and to award its
confidence only for its own benefit.

BUFFON

A Fox was boasting to a Cat of its clever devices for escaping its enemies. "I have a whole bag of tricks," he said, "which contains a hundred ways of escaping my enemies."

"I have only one," said the Cat; "but I can generally manage with that." Just at that moment they heard the cry of a pack of hounds coming towards them, and the Cat immediately scampered up a tree and hid herself in the boughs. "This is my plan," said the Cat. "What are you going to do?" The Fox thought first of one way, then of another, and while he was debating the hounds came nearer and nearer, and at last the Fox in his confusion was caught up by the hounds and soon killed by the huntsmen. Miss Puss, who had been looking on, said: "Better one safe way than a hundred on which you cannot reckon."

AESOP'S FABLES

THE FOX AND THE CAT

Do you think it's easy to be a cat? Do you really think so? Yeah, you're right!

GARFIELD

My cats, I don't know if they live with me. I live with them. They have access to all the rooms. Living together, we meet very often. We brush against each other.

BERNARD PIVOT

In its presence, the seconds stretch out, lazy and indolent. Time falls in step with the cat.

HERVÉ DESBOIS

Since each of us is blessed with only one life, why not live it with a cat?

ROBERT STEARNS

A cat pours his body on the floor like water. It is restful just to see him.

WILLIAM LYON PHELPS

Cats are never bored, unlike dogs...
But never forget to leave them something to eat, drink, and play with!

HERVÉ DESBOIS

But how could we think of holding against roses this wonderful defence mechanism we dread in cats?

CHAMPFLEURY

There is a witch cat. Very black, it has the power to bring wealth to the person who adopts and appreciates it.

LEGEND OF THE SOUTH OF FRANCE

The body coils up, settles down, the head comes to rest on a paw, the tail curls up around a thigh. Only an ear is moving, then stops. Total peace rises up from this inert ball of fur, lost in the deepest of sleeps.

PIERRE DARMANGEAT

What greater gift than the love of a cat?

CHARLES DICKENS

They are called heretics because they hide in places where no one finds them, just like cats.

FRANCISCAN MONK IN THE MIDDLE AGES

When I look back on my life, I have regrets. So many lost years! All this time spent awake!

GARFIELD

Cats contaminate not only with their brains, but also with their hair, breath and look...

AMBROISE PARÉ

Minnaloushe creeps through the grass
From moonlit place to place,
The sacred moon overhead
Has taken a new phase.
Does Minnaloushe know that his pupils
Will pass from change to change,
And that from round to crescent,
From crescent to round they range?
Minnaloushe creeps through the grass
Alone, important and wise,
And lifts to the changing moon
His changing eyes.

WILLIAM BUTLER YEATS
THE CAT AND THE MOON

You look "like the cat that got the cream", or you look quite proud of yourself.

ENGLISH EXPRESSION

The sun rose slowly, like a fiery furball coughed up uneasily onto a sky-blue carpet by a giant unseen cat.

MICHAEL MCGAREL

Cat chronicles: In America, Pennsylvania was where ratter cats were imported, around 1749, to protect colonies battling with thousands of black rats.

LAURETTE THERRIEN

A cat creates its own routes in your apartment, which it transforms into a territory where it has its playing areas, its favourite walls (to the wallpapers' great dismay), and its privileged resting areas, depending on the time of day or night.

VIVRE AVEC SON CHAT

Meow is like aloha — it can mean anything.

HANK KETCHUM

We cannot without becoming cats, perfectly understand the cat mind.

ST. GEORGE MIVART

For a long time, an artist I have been.
How many plays, how many stories written
In my honour
For my pleasure?
Puss in Boots and The Aristocats
By Jean Françaix, Les Demoiselles de la Nuit,
Footlight Parade by mister Bacon Lloyd,
And the famous Cats by Webber, Andrew Lloyd.

HERVÉ DESBOIS
CHRONIQUES DE CHATS

Cats are inquisitive, but hate to admit it.

MASON COOLEY

Cat chronicles: All through his life, Chateaubriand always remained faithful to cats. His wife had in fact nicknamed him "The Cat".

LAURETTE THERRIEN

If your cat is being a rascal, a little flick on the nose, pretend to ignore it, it's better than a good thrashing!

Excerpt from
GUIDE VÉTÉRINAIRE DES CHIENS ET DES CHATS

It like the fact that cats are mysterious, and it's probably this character trait which makes them so popular, or makes people hate them: they are different.

PIERRE DARMANGEAT

Cat chronicles: Canada is where naked cats are bred. Isn't that peculiar for a country with endless winters?

LAURETTE THERRIEN

If, for yourself you prepare some fish
For your cat's sake, don't be selfish
Don't forget to leave him a portion
Or it'll be sulking, with reason!

HERVÉ DESBOIS

In a cat's eye, all things belong to cats.

ENGLISH PROVERB

Way down deep, we're all motivated by the same urges. Cats have the courage to live by them.

JIM DAVIS

Cat chronicles:
When the Persians, by tactic, tied cats to their shields, the Egyptians capitulated, incapable of hurting these sacred animals.

LAURETTE THERRIEN

Even the stupidest cat seems to know more than any dog.

ELEANOR CLARK

Lighten the small boat of life, and equip it with the only things you need: a simple interior and simple pleasures, one or two friends who deserve to be called friends, someone you love and who loves you – a cat, a dog, a pipe or two – bring enough supplies to feed and clothe your-self, a little more than is necessary to quench your thirst, thirst being a terrible thing...

JEROME K. JEROME

A metaphysician is a man who, at midnight, goes into a dark cave without a light, looking for a black cat which isn't there.

LORD CHARLES SYNGE BOWEN

By associating with the cat, one only risks becoming richer.

COLETTE

How can one live with a stuffed cat? It's the height of tastelessness.

ZOÉ VALDÈS

What is the link between the eyes of a cat and a camera? Both focus according to the light's intensity.

LAURETTE THERRIEN

A rutting cat or a cat in heat listen only to its sexual urges, and has only one idea in its head: to go court the girlfriend and give a good thrashing to the loser hanging about its territory, or go tantalise the neighbouring cats and drive them up the wall!

EXCERPT FROM VIVRE AVEC SON CHAT

Kittens are born with their eyes shut. They open them in about six days, take a look around, then close them again for the better part of their lives.

STEPHEN BAKER

I prefer dogs to cats, and all felines remind me of that upon the first look – a piercing and grudging look.

JAMES THURBER

Cat or undertaker?
Over there, in my Finland
I am in charge of transporting
The souls of the dead across the moor
All the way to the distant kingdom of the dead.

HERVÉ DESBOIS

ADAPTATION OF OLD FINNISH FOLKLORE

Nature breaks through the eyes of the cat.

IRISH PROVERB

He gives you a wave of his long brown tail
Which says: 'I'll see you again!
You'll meet without fail on the Midnight Mail
The Cat of the Railway Train.'

T. S. ELIOT

You can not look at a sleeping cat and feel tense.

JANE PAULEY

God created the cat so man would know the
pleasure of stroking the tiger.

JOSEPH MÉRY

That's the life of a gutter cat. Some days, I tell you, it really is hell!

CHANTALE LANDRY

SA MAJESTÉ DES GOUTTIÈRES

If you are a "bag of cats" in the morning, you woke up in a foul mood.

ENGLISH EXPRESSION

Cats are lucky: darkness doesn't stop them from reading.

LOUIS SCUTENAIRE

A cat has nine lives. For three he plays, for three he strays, and for the last three he stays.

ENGLISH PROVERB

It was a beautiful Egyptian cat, long, powerful, and the colour of sand. She seemed to be born out of darkness itself.

DANIEL PENNAC

CABOT-CABOCHE

It is tame, meaning it accepts us as companions, but not domesticated: it is neither "humanised", nor "de-natured". The cat is cat, and that state is more than enough for it.

PIERRE DARMANGEAT

Cats don't catch mice to please Khoda (God).

AFGAN PROVERB

He was only a cat. He hadn't understood that we don't die of love: we live off it.

BERNADETTE RENAUD

LE CHAT DE L'ORATOIRE

An old cat will not learn how to dance.

MOROCCAN PROVERB

Once I'm on a stride of not doing too much, it's hard to stop.

GARFIELD

There are two means of refuge from the miseries of life: music and cats.

ALBERT SCHWEITZER

Children remind me that life can be everywhere, in the sweet-smelling blade of grass, in the cat we stroke, or in the short-lived snowman.

HERVÉ DESBOIS

A cat may look at a king.

ENGLISH PROVERB

In the time of the Flood, Lady Mouse and her numerous descendants were starting to tackle the food stocks, and Noah was getting much worried about it. Not knowing what to do, he addressed a fervent prayer to God, which had the effect of making the lion who was passing by sneeze twice. From his dilated nostrils came two cats who immediately took it upon themselves to chase the mice.
The Almighty had just answered a great need by creating the cat, and had saved the Ark from famine.

PIERRE DARMANGEAT

Happy owner, happy cat. Indifferent owner, reclusive cat.

CHINESE PROVERB

You never choose a cat: it chooses you.

PHILIPPE RAGUENEAU

Cat chronicles: In Spain, one pillar of the Tarragon Cathedral's cloister, dating from the XIIIth and XIVth centuries, shows a procession in which rats bury cats pretending to be dead.

LAURETTE THERRIEN

The phrase "domestic cat" is an oxymoron.

GEORGE F. WILL

I consider it to be a feline characteristic, nobody can do anything about it. sometimes it's imperative that I do nothing.

GARFIELD

Cats are there to teach us that on earth, not everything has a purpose.

GARRISON KEILLOR

If you think you're the "cat's meow", you have quite an overrated opinion of yourself.

ENGLISH EXPRESSION

People who like cats love this independence they have, because it guarantees their own freedom.

ANNY DUPEREY

Aggressive cat, cat full of spirit, signs of vitality. Have fun, amuse it for a moment, intensely, it will be rid of its excess energy.

Excerpt from
GUIDE VÉTÉRINAIRE DES CHIENS ET DES CHATS

By the way, do cats eat bats?

LEWIS CARROLL

Happy is the home with at least one cat.

ITALIAN PROVERB

A cat that plays is already in good health. A cat that plays finds its own balance, and reinforces this balance in sleep.

Excerpt from
VIVRE AVEC SON CHAT

A black cat hides in its pelt one immaculate white hair. He who finds it and pull it out without being scratched has then the most precious lucky charm!

LEGEND OF THE LOWLANDS

Scritching the bark
Of the sycamore-tree,
She's reached her ark
And's hissing at me

ELEANOR FARJEON

If we treated everyone we meet with the same affection we bestow upon our favourite cat, they, too, would purr.

MARTIN BUXBAUM

The cat was created when the lion sneezed.

ARABIAN PROVERB

"Has the cat got your tongue?", or have you lost the ability to talk?

ENGLISH EXPRESSION

Come, here is the cat stroking its paw over its ear. It will rain again tomorrow.

MARCEL AYMÉ

LES CONTES DU CHAT PERCHÉ

He wanted a dog, she wanted a cat. Both animals, still babies, were therefore adopted on the same day. The German shepherd was well over twenty times the size of the kitten, but a few days later, both ate out of the same bowl, the cat waiting for the dog to come near before starting its meal.

LAURETTE THERRIEN

I gave an order to a cat, and the cat gave it to its tail.

CHINESE PROVERB

To please your cat
Cook him some liver
Chicken livers, two or three
His chops he'll be licking!

HERVÉ DESBOIS

Cats are poetry in motion.

JIM DAVIS

Cats and superstition: some maintain that cats, by climbing on ship masts, drive away the wandering souls who haunt the waves for all eternity.

LAURETTE THERRIEN

Cats, flies and women are ever at their toilets.

FRENCH PROVERB

Cats do not have to be shown how to have a good time, for they are unfailing ingenious in that respect.

JAMES MASON

Cat chronicles: In the Xth century, in Wales, a champion ratter cat is worth a fourteen-day-old colt, a six-month-old calf, or a pig, completely weaned.

FERNAND MÉRY

Cats, although they do climb easily, don't know how to come back down.

LAURETTE THERRIEN

A cat doesn't listen to words; it listens to voices, it's safer.

BERNADETTE RENAUD
LE CHAT DE L'ORATOIRE

When you're being too nosy, beware: "Curiosity killed the cat!"

ENGLISH EXPRESSION

Cat: discreet and silent companion that watches us live without judging us.

HERVÉ DESBOIS

In Ancient Egypt
I was goddess of the sun
And later my cult
Was that of the moon.
I am cat, and goddess,
Adored by my priestesses.
I am Bastet, feline divinity
But full of femininity.

HERVÉ DESBOIS

Cats, who were deified in Ancient Egypt, were demonised during the Middle Ages.

LAURETTE THERRIEN

Why run when I can watch
With infinite patience
Then startlingly, and in silence
My prey finally catch?

HERVÉ DESBOIS

A domestic animal, if ever there were some, the cat nevertheless stays partly mysterious.

PIERRE DARMANGEAT

In order to keep a good perspective of his own importance, each person should have a dog who adores them and a cat who ignores them.

DEREKE BRUCE

You see, cat, the guard only judged with his eyes, and didn't understand anything.

BERNADETTE RENAUD

LE CHAT DE L'ORATOIRE

If he whips my cats, a ghost will come and persecute him.

GEORGES BRASSENS

When rats infest the Palace a lame cat is better than the swiftest horse.

CHINESE PROVERB

Dogs are the instrument chosen by God to tell us there is worse than us.

GARFIELD

By separating kittens from their mothers too early, they risk being excessively attached to their human companions, and becoming "fusion-cats".

LAURETTE THERRIEN

Some people say that cats are sneaky, evil, and cruel. True, and they have many other fine qualities as well.

MISSY DIZICK

Who can believe that there is no soul behind those luminous eyes!

THÉOPHILE GAUTIER

Cats are autocrats of naked self-interest. They are both amoral and immoral, consciously breaking rules.

CAMILLE PAGLIA

We Indians of the Kauri tribe
Far in the south of Peru
Believe that all our lives
And our wildest dreams
Depend only on him
Ccoa, the great cat god.
In the mountains he lives
And lightening he sends us
Come harvest time
When his offerings he wants
To soothe his passions
And give us blue skies again

HERVÉ DESBOIS

ADAPTATION OF A PERUVIAN LEGEND

Cat chronicles: During the Middle Ages, in sea ports, we find cat shops where ship crews come to stock up with ratter cats.

LAURETTE THERRIEN

The Persian cat has the reputation of being very gentle and of getting along very well with children. We seldom meet its claws, and if it seems indifferent, it is only being modest, because it has a real need for affection.

EXCERPT FROM VIVRE AVEC SON CHAT

In the superior order of things, each must have his role to play. Mine is to sleep!

GARFIELD

When a cat cries over a rat, it's a case of false compassion.

CHINESE PROVERB

Cats and superstition: In the Middle Ages, witches often had black cats as pets, and people said that these women had the power to take the form of a cat.

LE GRAND LIVRE DES CHATS

Cat chronicles: In Beni-Hassan, in the mid XVIII^{Th} century, a immense feline cemetery was found: three hundred thousand embalmed and mummified cats.

LAURETTE THERRIEN

But the cat is grown small and thin with desire,
Transformed to a creeping lust for milk.

HAROLD MONRO

I have as a companion a big grey-red cat with black stripes across it. It was born in the Vatican, in Raphael's dressing room. Leon XII had raised it in a fold of his robe where I often saw it with envy, when the Pontiff granted me an audience... We nicknamed it: "the Pope's cat."

CHATEAUBRIAND

Once a year, at the top of the Cinq-Chemins, cats get together to make pancakes.

LEGEND OF THE POITOU-CHARENTES

Sorrow is a sort of wild cat, grey in colour. Its cry is rather sad and mournful. Many must come together to overcome it. As, alone, one has difficulty in driving sorrow away.

FRANCIS BLANCHE

Fortunately, my cat was found this morning, otherwise I would have hung myself!

FATHER GALLIANI

Today Thailand, yesterday old Siam country, that is where I come from, an animal once sacred, I am the Siamese cat.

HERVÉ DESBOIS

A home without a cat – and a well-fed, well-petted and properly revered cat – may be a home, perhaps, but how can it prove title?

MARK TWAIN

A cat is not stroked. It strokes itself with my hand, with my knee, with whatever it wishes.

PIERRE DESPROGES

There is "more than one way to skin a cat", or there are many ways to perform a task.

ENGLISH EXPRESSION

Authors like cats because they are such quiet, loveable, wise creatures, and cats like authors for the same reasons.

ROBERTSON DAVIES

Cats look beyond appearances – beyond species entirely, it seems – to peer into the heart.

BARBARA L. DIAMOND

My husband said it was him or the cat... I miss him sometimes.

UNKNOWN

"Si'La" I am called.
I am a demon
Who plays with your life
Like a cat plays with a mouse.
Traveller, do not get lost
Because on your way
I am the one you shall find.
Until death you shall dance
To the flute music you will hear
I will play it for you alone.

HERVÉ DESBOIS

ADAPTATION OF AN OLD LEGEND

There is no proof that the flea that lives on the
mouse fears the cat.

HENRI MICHAUX

I'm the only cat of my kind.
I'm king of the highway
Prince of the boulevard
Duke of the avant-garde
The world is my backyard

TOM ROWE
THE ARISTOCATS

All May cats are bad.

ORIENTAL PROVERB

Cities, like cats, will reveal themselves at night.

RUPERT BROOKE

Cats are excellent comedians, great masters at striking the right chords. If they can't talk, they know how to be melodramatic using their vocal chords with unequalled brio!

HERVÉ DESBOIS

Two things are aesthetically perfect in the world - the clock and the cat.

ÉMILE-AUGUSTE CHARTIER

A happy arrangement: many people prefer cats to other people, and many cats prefer people to other cats.

MASON COOLEY

I'm exhausted just thinking about being in a vertical position.

GARFIELD

A kitten buried in the ground rids it of all weeds.

LOW-PYRENEES SAYING

But what is behind those eyes intensely set on empty space? What meditation do they express? What dream? Regret of freedom? Desire to escape? Void...?

PIERRE DARMANGEAT

One cat just leads to another.

ERNEST HEMINGWAY

We say: at night, all cats are grey. Wrong: all cats are sleeping.

PATRICK TIMSIT

Cat chronicles: During the XXIInd dynasty, the Egyptians put cats in charge of watching over the temples; the cat was later deified.

LAURETTE THERRIEN

You don't own a cat, a cat owns you.

FRANÇOISE GIROUX

Dogs bark, cats meow, because it's in their nature. As for me, I philosophise, it's my nature, it's as spontaneous and involuntary and has no more importance to it.

ALEXANDRA DAVID-NEEL

Aesop tells of how Venus accepted to transform into a woman a cat in love with a handsome young man. Unfortunately, the woman remained so much catlike that a single mouse was enough to pull her out of the marriage bed during their lovemaking.

GREEK MYTHOLOGY

I am the God of the Mochicas,
Whatever my form may be,
Yesterday cat, today man,
"Ai Apaec" I am called,
Their greatest god.
I live among my people
With a dog as my friend
And a lizard as servant.
I am a master in life
And a master of all lives.
I have defeated demons and serpents
And I protect men, women, and children.

HERVÉ DESBOIS

ADAPTATION OF A PERUVIAN MYTHOLOGY

Cat chronicles: Egyptian women dreamt of resembling cats with the strangeness of their eyes, the obliquity of their look, the suppleness of their waist and their feverish abandon.

LAURETTE THERRIEN

Working on the assumption that an imbecile is rarely curious, we can think that the cat is intelligent.

PIERRE DARMANGEAT

I think that this forehead against forehead contact is the superior manifestation of tenderness in cats.

ANNY DUPEREY

Cats communicate with each other, and definitely reason.

MONTAIGNE

A cat's dreams are full of mice.

LIBANESE PROVERB

One day, Henry De Montherlant asked a young girl if there was a reason why she had not given names to all the cats living in her home. "How do you call them? – I don't call them," she answered, "they come when they want to."

CAT CHRONICLES

To gain a cat's friendship is a difficult thing to do.

THÉOPHILE GAUTIER

You can't own a cat. The best you can do is be partners.

SIR HARRY SWANSON

She was occupied in knitting; a large cat sat demurely at her feet; nothing in short was wanting to complete the beau-ideal of domestic comfort.

CHARLOTTE BRONTË

JANE EYRE

Everybody wants to be a cat
Because a cat's the only cat
Who knows where it's at
When playin' jazz he always has
A welcome mat
'Cause everybody digs a swingin' cat

THE ARISTOCATS

Cats certainly like to feel we are calm, not too fidgety, and to see a human stay in the same place for a long time wins their trust and they can settle next to who works this way.

ANNY DUPEREY

The epitome of peace is a sitting cat.

JULES RENARD

Cat chronicles: The great prophet Mohammed cut a sleeve off his burnous so he wouldn't disturb his cat Muessa while it slept. Why? Because he loved it.

LAURETTE THERRIEN

To understand a cat, you must realise that he has his own gifts, his own viewpoint, even his own morality.

LILIAN JACKSON BRAUN

Cats never give up on catching mice.

GERMAN PROVERB

"When the cat is away, the mice will play", or the subordinate become emancipated when the master is not there.

ENGLISH EXPRESSION

Each cat has two sides: lazy and bold. Sadly, "bold" doesn't live here anymore.

GARFIELD

A house without a cat is like a winter without snow.

HERVÉ DESBOIS

Cat chronicles: A creature similar to the weasel, the Miacis, lived on earth during the Eocene era, some 50 million years ago. Countless generations of carnivores come from this ferocious and ingenious prehistoric creature. We can recognise it as the ancestor of our domestic cats, which are endowed with the same survival skills.

EXCERPT FROM LE GRAND LIVRE DES CHATS

"Well, then," the Cat went on, "you see, a dog growls when it's angry, and wags its tail when it's pleased. Now I growl when I'm pleased, and wag my tail when I'm angry. Therefore I'm mad."

LEWIS CARROLL

You do not speak, and still your eyes say so much. Not a word, only strokes, and through licks and purrs, you tell me all your affection.

HERVÉ DESBOIS

If you give yourself a "cat's lick", there's a good chance you'll still be dirty after this half-hearted wash.

ENGLISH EXPRESSION

Cats and superstition: We find many three-coloured cats aboard Japanese ships, because they have the reputation of being able to predict storms.

LAURETTE THERRIEN

Tut, never fear me: I am as vigilant as a cat to steal cream.

SHAKESPEARE

I love to sleep! How would we be without sleep? Probably very tired.

GARFIELD

There is only need of a few things to make a cat happy: good food and fresh water, good moments of play and good naps, attention and petting, and, of course, elementary care...

EXCERPT FROM VIVRE AVEC SON CHAT

I am not a kangaroo
Nor a hare or a rabbit
I am a real tomcat
From a beautiful and distant land
I go by jumps even when I run
I am the cat of the Isle of Man.

HERVÉ DESBOIS
CHRONIQUES DE CHATS

The cat became a great lord, and thereafter ran after mice only for entertainment.

PERRAULT
PUSS IN BOOTS

Cat chronicles: In India, for hundreds of years, the orthodox Hindu rite demanded of believers that they raise and feed at least one cat per family.

LAURETTE THERRIEN

Cats and superstition: Woe betide you if some black cat enters your home, drive it out without delay, because it is not an omen of good fortune.

SICILY

The thing is that a cat, in its life, always meets a dog it can no longer live without. It finds it difficult to put up with all the other dogs, but that dog, it loves it: that's how it is.

DANIEL PENNAC, CABOT-CABOCHE

The dog wakes up three times to watch over its master; the cat wakes up three times to strangle it.

CREUSE SAYING

The impassive feline stares at the man.

BERNADETTE RENAUD

LE CHAT DE L'ORATOIRE

Pussy will rub my knees with her head
Pretending she loves me hard;
But the very minute I go to my bed
Pussy runs out in the yard

RUDYARD KIPLING

Bursts of frenzy, moments of dead calm... Cats are a phenomenon. Capable of an incredible profusion of energy, they are lazy beings who claim their laziness loud and clear!

EXCERPT FROM VIVRE AVEC SON CHAT

When the aviator Ruth Edler attempted her transatlantic crossing, she brought with her a stuffed Felix the Cat.

HERVÉ DESBOIS

Jogging is a disease. I'm the vaccine.

GARFIELD

Cat chronicles:
I am called Abyssinian
Similar to the Ethiopian wild cat
But from another land I come
Since from England I am.

HERVÉ DESBOIS

Cat chronicles: Madame de Staël, during her incarceration in the Bastille, discovers (at the same time as mice) the cat's skills, and, while admitting that up until then she had never cared for these beasts, deigns to speak of them nobly.

LAURETTE THERRIEN

You can keep a dog; but it is the cat who keeps people, because cats find humans useful domestic animals.

GEORGE MIKES

Don't hesitate to throw the cat out of the kitchen, because whatever it finds, it won't hesitate.

IBANEZ

I can't help it, it's hard for me to confide entirely in someone who doesn't like cats.

EDMOND JALOUX

There's a funny little cat
With a tummy nice and fat.
He's won picture fame . . .
Felix is his name.
Has a funny little walk
Whiskers on his chin [. . .]
He's so full of funny tricks,
Fed some sawdust to the chicks,
Now instead of eggs . . .
They lay table legs.

ED E. BRYANT

FELIX KEPT ON WALKING

As anyone who has ever been around a cat for any length of time well knows cats have enormous patience with the limitations of the human kind.

CLEVELAND AMORY

An ordinary kitten will ask more questions than any five-year-old.

CARL VAN VECHTEN

No matter how much the world changes, cats will not lay eggs.

AFRICAN PROVERB

I sometimes let go of everything for a short while. I let go of time, I stop running like a madman and I lie down in front of my cat.
I stay there, doing nothing but looking at it, sometimes venturing into brushing its fur, as if to immerse myself in its feline softness. And magic sets in…
I feel the stress that filled me evaporate in long, lazy breaths, as if its own rhythm was filling me, driving away all of the present moment's worries.

HERVÉ DESBOIS

According to scientists who study their behaviour, cats spend about two thirds of their lives sleeping. What a dog's life!

HERVÉ DESBOIS

Life will go on for ever
with all that cat can wish
warmth and the glad procession
of fish and milk and fish.

ALEXANDER GRAY

Of all God's creatures, there is only one that cannot be made slave of the leash. That one is the cat. If man could be crossed with the cat it would improve the man, but it would deteriorate the cat.

MARK TWAIN